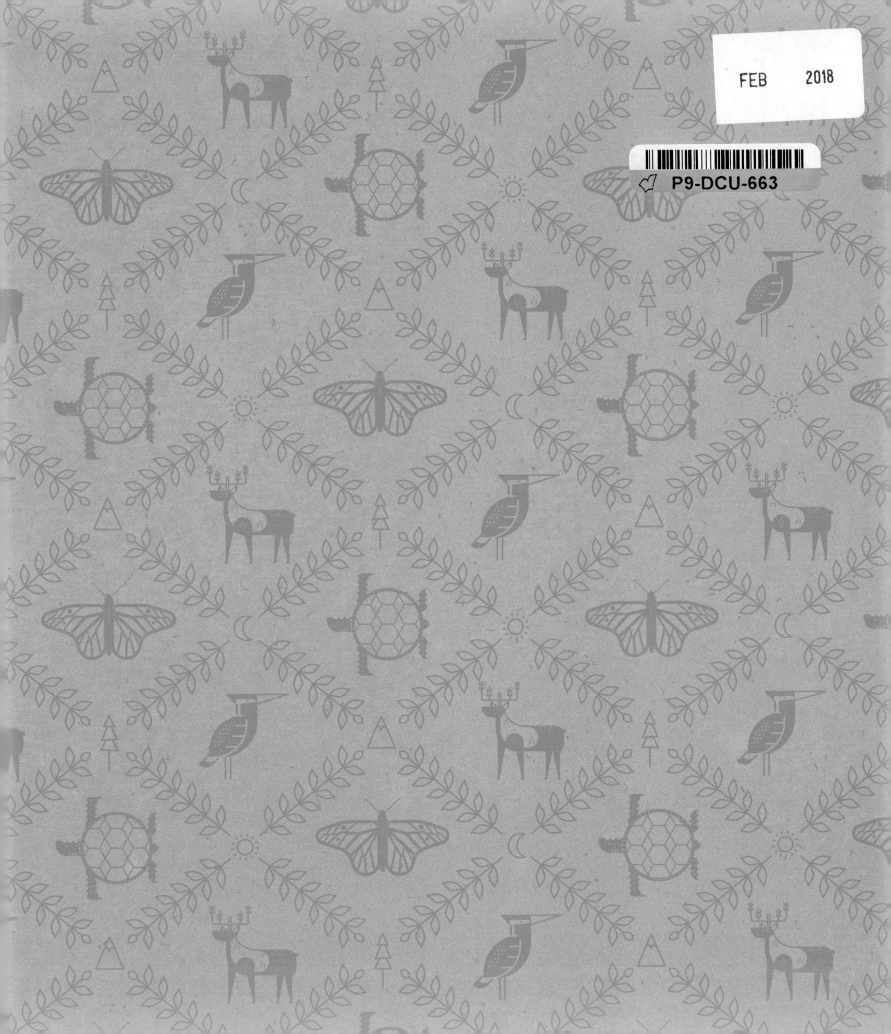

STERLING CHILDREN'S BOOKS

New York

An Imprint of Sterling Publishing Co., Inc.
1166 Avenue of the Americas
New York, NY 10036

STERLING CHILDREN'S BOOKS and the distinctive Sterling Children's Books logo
are trademarks of Sterling Publishing Co., Inc.

© 2017 by Egmont Limited

First Sterling edition published in 2017.
First published in Great Britain in 2017 by Red Shed,
an imprint of Egmont UK Limited
www.egmont.co.uk

ISBN: 978-1-4549-2518-7

For information about custom editions, special sales, and premium and
corporate purchases, please contact Sterling Special Sales at 800-805-5489
or specialsales@sterlingpublishing.com.

Manufactured in Malaysia
Lot #:
2 4 6 8 10 9 7 5 3 1
04/17

www.sterlingpublishing.com

AROUND THE WORLD IN NUMBERS

CLIVE GIFFORD   JOSH HURLEY

STERLING CHILDREN'S BOOKS
New York

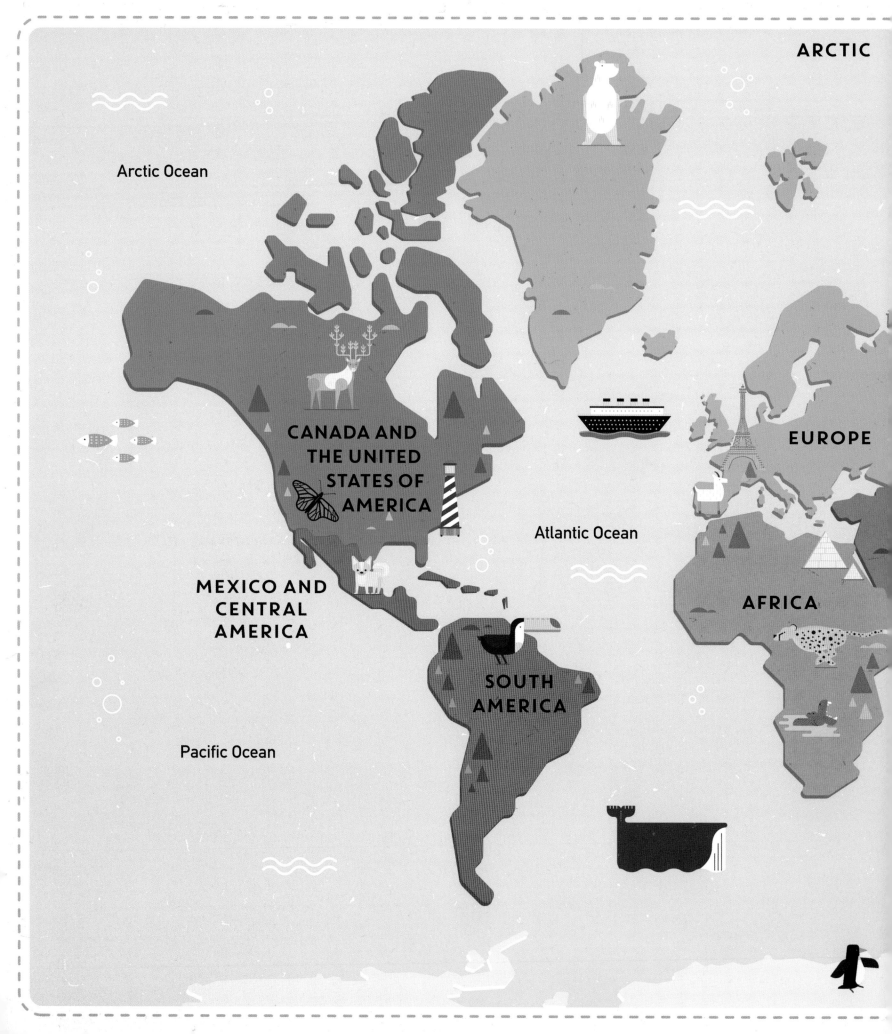

Arctic Ocean

CANADA AND
THE UNITED
STATES OF
AMERICA

MEXICO AND
CENTRAL
AMERICA

Atlantic Ocean

EUROPE

AFRICA

SOUTH
AMERICA

Pacific Ocean

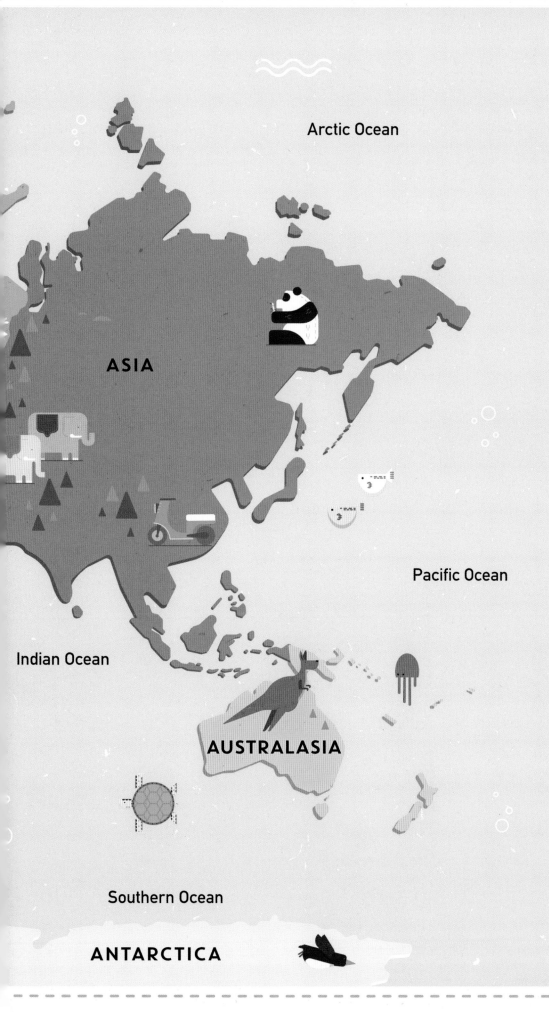

Arctic Ocean

ASIA

Indian Ocean

Pacific Ocean

AUSTRALASIA

Southern Ocean

ANTARCTICA

CONTENTS

EUROPE

Grab your suitcase and fill it with facts as you travel through the different countries that make up Europe. Packed with over 740 million people, there are lots of enormous and tiny numbers to discover, as well as some really surprising ones.

1,500 paintbrushes and 66 tons of paint are used when the Eiffel Tower in Paris, France, is repainted every 7 years.

33 pounds of sausages were paid by a Romanian soccer club in 2006 as a transfer fee for striker Marius Cioara.

36 trap doors in the arena of the Colosseum of ancient Rome in Italy were opened to let out lions and tigers to do battle with gladiators or defenceless slaves.

54,250 tennis balls are used during the Wimbledon tennis tournament held every year in London, England.

40,000 interlocking columns of basalt rock make up the Giant's Causeway on the coast of northeast Ireland.

84,000 storks live in Poland – around a fifth of all the storks there are in the world.

1,430

miles is the distance that migrating noctule bats fly in late summer each year when they migrate from Russia south to winter in Romania.

32,810

feet is how high the Icelandic volcano Eyjafjallajökull sent volcanic ash into the air when it erupted in 2010. About 20 European countries had to close their airspace.

36,000

pieces of LEGO are produced every minute by the LEGO factory in Billund, Denmark.

100,000 flights were cancelled because of the ash in the air.

13,980

feet up, near the top of the continent's highest mountain, Mont Blanc, is the highest toilet in Europe.

3,280

feet can be climbed in just 15 minutes by the Chamois goats that live in the high Pyrenees mountains of France and Spain.

53

mountains in the Alps of central Europe have been climbed by a beagle dog called Tschingel, the only dog to be voted a member of the exclusive Alpine Club.

Building Marvels

You cannot build bridges, towers, homes, or other buildings without knowing your numbers. Did you know, for example, that it took an incredible 40,690 tons of steel to build the Petronas Towers in Malaysia – more than the weight of 8,200 monster trucks?

1,500,000

recycled green and brown glass bottles were used by Buddhist monks to build a large temple complex called Wat Pa Maha Chedi Kaew in Thailand.

696

feet above the sea is the helipad of the Burj Al Arab hotel in Dubai. Designed to resemble a billowing sail, the hotel has 202 luxury suites and when lit up at night is said to represent both water and fire.

1,300

oak trees were used for the beams of the Notre Dame cathedral in the French city of Paris. That's equal to about 52 acres of forest.

The 420-ft-long Notre Dame cathedral is visited by 13 million people every year.

3 bedrooms make up the sleeping area of the Nautilus House in Mexico City, built in the shape of a sea snail, with smooth, spiralling walls. It was created by architect Javier Senosiain.

4 is the number of years it took to build the Dancing House in Prague – between 1992 and 1996. It is a symbol of modern architecture and has a restaurant on the top floor.

2 construction groups built the Petronas twin towers in Malaysia. They took one tower each, racing each other to the top. Each floor had to be built in only four days!

The towers are 88 stories high, with a further 5 floors underground.

3.99 degrees is the amount the Tower of Pisa tilts, leaning 12.8 feet from its base.

This Italian bell tower was completed in 1372. It weighs nearly 15,980 tons.

2,890 feet is the distance in 1999 that the Cape Hatteras lighthouse was moved away from the the ocean in North Carolina.

The move took 23 days.

315 skyscrapers (buildings over 492 feet tall) have been erected in Hong Kong – more than in any other city in the world.

ASIA

This continent is not only home to the world's highest mountain, Mount Everest, but also contains the two countries with the most people, China and India. More than half of all the people in the world live in Asia.

18

feet is the length of one of the eyebrows of the Leshan Giant Buddha in China. This gigantic 233-ft-high statue with its 22-ft-tall ears was carved over 1,200 years ago.

52,000

pupils attended the City Montessori school in the Indian city of Lucknow in 2015. It is the largest school in the world with 1,050 classrooms.

38,000,000

motorbikes are the most popular form of transport in Vietnam. They are an affordable way of getting around a country that has less than three million car owners.

Covering an area bigger than 180 soccer fields, Angkor Wat is the biggest religious site in the world.

6,000

elephants were used 900 years ago to help build the majestic Angkor Wat temple complex in Cambodia.

Pandas have to eat 26–84 lbs of bamboo every day to get enough nutrients.

1,864

giant pandas are believed to be the only ones living in the wild in China, according to a major survey carried out in 2014.

21 is the number of times a Nepalese man called Apa Sherpa has reached the very top of Mount Everest. No one has reached the peak more times than Apa!

8.8 tons of rubbish were brought down Mount Everest in 2012, including climbing gear and the remains of an old helicopter. Almost a fifth of it was turned into artwork.

234 climbers reached the summit of Mount Everest on a single day – May 19, 2012.

The waste was carried down by 65 people and 75 yaks.

9.5 inches is the diameter of one of the world's largest pearls. Discovered off the coast of the Philippines in the 1930s, the Pearl of Lao Tzu weighs a whopping 14.1 lbs.

4,409,000 pounds of fish and other seafood is bought and sold in Tokyo's Tsukiji Market in Japan every day. It is thought to be the biggest fish market in the world.

6,852 is the number of islands that make up the nation of Japan. Less than 500 are inhabited.

Four islands – Honshu, Hokkaido, Kyushu and Shikoku – make up 97 percent of Japan's land area.

150 inches is the leg span of the gigantic Japanese spider crab which is found in the waters around the coast of Japan's southern islands.

AFRICA

Africa is a fascinating continent that contains more than 1.2 billion people living in 54 countries and speaking more than 2,000 different languages. It is a continent of extremes, from vast hot deserts to lush wet jungles and large plains packed with wildlife.

27.9

is the number of twins for every 1,000 children born in the African nation of Benin. It is the highest twin birth rate in the world.

2,000,000

people live in the Sahara Desert. This vast desert, which covers a quarter of all of Africa, is the same size as the USA, where 300,000,000 people live.

500

teeth filled the mouth of Nigersaurus, a strange kind of dinosaur. The teeth mowed grass for food. Fossils of this dinosaur, along with the 36-foot-long prehistoric SuperCroc, were found in Niger.

1,844

movies were produced in Nigeria in 2013. Nigeria's film industry is nicknamed Nollywood and makes more movies every year than Hollywood in the USA.

7,800

waste plastic drinks bottles, filled with sand, were used to build a house in Yelwa, Nigeria, in 2011. The clever design saves waste and was cheap to construct.

3,106.75

is the number of carats of the world's biggest diamond, the Cullinan, when discovered in South Africa in 1905. To give an idea of its size and worth, a 15-carat diamond ring could cost over $1 million today!

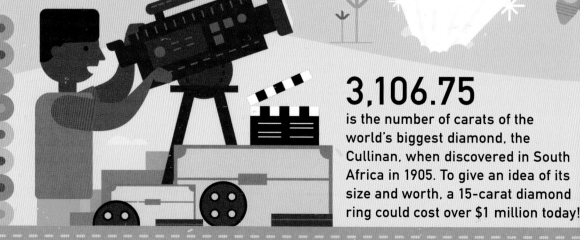

243.4

pounds of pure gold was used to make the inner coffin of Tutankhamun, the ancient Egyptian pharaoh. Tutankhamun's tomb contained riches including chariots, sandals and more than 5,000 other objects.

Many of the sandals had pictures of Tut's enemies etched on the soles so that as he walked, he trampled them!

1,000

is the estimated number of different species of fish found in Lake Malawi – the most diverse lake in the world.

2.25

gallons of water can be held in an African elephant's trunk at one time. The trunk is strong enough to push down trees but can also pick up a single piece of straw.

2,443

was the number of times poor Johannes Relleke was stung by bees in 1962. He jumped into the River Gwaii to escape the bees, and survived.

100,000,000

leather slippers are made in cobblers' shops in Morocco every year, most of them in the winding streets of the historic city of Fez.

300

individual nests can make up a community of social weaver birds. They work together to weave single nests into a colony that can be as large as 26.25 by 6.56 feet.

The nests can grow so large that they hold 100 nesting chambers for up to 400 chicks!

Animals and Nature

Nature is packed with numbers, from the 50 billion chickens on the planet to the fewer than 100 Sumatran rhinos that survive. Other nature numbers relate to body parts, from the 8 fingers and 4 thumbs on a mole's front paws to a millipede that has 750 legs!

10

sets of antlers are grown and shed by a mountain caribou in its lifetime. Canada is home to about 2.4 million of these creatures.

20

is the number of times per second that a woodpecker's beak may hit a tree when it pecks. The bird's beak hits the tree at a speed of 14.9 miles per hour.

Woodpeckers may peck up to 12,000 times in a single day searching for food.

3

steps is all it takes for a cheetah to go from standing still to sprinting at 37 miles per hour.

The cheetah is the world's fastest land animal and can reach speeds of over 59 mph in short bursts.

32

muscles in each ear allow cats to move their ears independently, pointing them in different directions to their body to catch all sounds.

1,500

babies are carried by some male seahorses in the pouches on their stomachs. Seahorses are the only species where the male takes over pregnancy from the female.

2.98 miles is the distance that the loud call of a howler monkey can travel through the rainforest in which it lives.

50 is the number of times its own bodyweight that a leafcutter ant can lift and carry.

2,000,000 visits to flowers must be made by bees in order to make enough honey in their hive to fill a small 16-ounce jar.

150 degrees is the widest angle that a hippopotamus can open its giant jaws to reveal its 19.7-inch-long teeth.

A 4.6ft-tall child could easily fit inside a hippo's open mouth!

243 pounds of dung are what an adult African elephant poops each day. It sounds like a lot but then the elephant eats a lot – as much as 309 pounds of food a day.

1 is the number of eyes a dolphin keeps open while it sleeps. Dolphins only rest one half of their brain when napping. The other half and one eye stays awake and alert so it can spot predators.

CANADA AND THE UNITED STATES OF AMERICA

Canada and the USA (United States of America) are two large countries in North America. Canada is the second biggest country in the world and shares an 5,520-mile-long border with the USA, the fourth largest nation on Earth.

1,305

feet is the distance that teenager Matt Suter was carried by a tornado in Fordland, Missouri in 2006. The 143 mile-per-hour winds threw him into the air, and he landed shaken and bruised but otherwise okay.

11,199,480

is the weight in pounds of the potato chips munched through by Americans on Super Bowl Sunday – the day of the final game of the National Football League.

Americans also eat 1.2 billion chicken wings and around 132 million pounds of avocados.

75

percent of a US one dollar bill is made of cotton. The rest is not made of paper but of linen. Each banknote weighs 0.35 ounces and is in circulation for between 18 months and five years.

508,000

solid gold bars, each weighing 28.7 pounds, were stored in special bank vaults 79 feet below the streets of New York in 2015. Over 90 percent of the gold is owned by countries or organizations outside the USA.

1,145

is the shoe size that the Statue of Liberty's 25-foot-long feet would take. Most women's shoe sizes in the USA are 6–9!

557,640

square feet is the amount that the island of Hawaii is getting bigger each year. Lava from the erupting Kilauea volcano hardens over time to form more rock.

2 people in each team take part in the Trenary Outhouse Classic in Michigan. They build an outdoor toilet that is complete with a toilet seat and toilet paper that is then raced along a course on skis.

15.5 miles per hour is the speed at which monarch butterflies fly when they migrate south each year from northern USA and southern Canada to California and Mexico for the winter.

5.9 million pounds of sticky maple syrup were stolen by thieves from a giant warehouse in Canada in 2012. The syrup was stored in large drums. Canada produces about three-quarters of the world's supply.

1.96 inches is the width of the 1,804 foot-long steel cable that tightrope walker Nik Wallenda used to walk across Niagara Falls in 2012. He had to carry his passport with him as his daredevil feat saw him cross the border from the USA to Canada.

2,789 is the length in feet of the world's largest beaver dam, in Wood Buffalo National Park, Canada. North American beavers make their dams out of tree branches and mud.

750 legs belong to the world record-holding California millipede known as *Illacme plenipes*. This insect was first discovered in 1926 but then not seen again until 2005.

Sports and Games

Sport is often about numbers and not just the score or the time of the fastest runner. From the most women's tennis titles (167 by Martina Navratilova), to the number of double stitches on a baseball (108), sports are packed with number facts.

79 feet were jumped by pro skateboarder Danny Way at the 2004 X Games – a new world record.

80 hours is how long US athlete Pamela Reed took to run across the state of Arizona without a nap.

206 miles per hour is the speed of a shuttlecock hit by Chinese badminton player Fu Haifeng in 2005. It is one of the fastest recorded speeds in a badminton match.

103 was the age of Gus Andreone in 2014 when he became the oldest golfer in the world to achieve a hole in one at a course in Florida.

91 inches is the height of Manute Bol, one of the tallest basketball players in history.

18 was the number of times Greek skier Antoin Miliordos fell over while attempting the ski slalom at the 1952 Winter Olympics.

900,000 is the number of baseballs used in each season by the 30 teams that make up Major League Baseball (MLB).

Antoin lost his balance near the end so he crossed the finishing line backward.

18 year-old Max Verstappen became the youngest driver to win a Formula 1 Grand Prix race in Spain in 2016.

249

miles is the height above Earth where the highest marathon took place. British astronaut Tim Peake ran 28.7 miles on a treadmill inside the International Space Station in 2016.

7 is the number of seconds it took for Italy's Emanuela Pierantozzi to beat Alexandra Schreiber at the 1992 Olympics – the fastest in women's judo history.

By contrast, Soona Lee-Tolley was just 5 years and 103 days old when she scored a hole in one in 2007.

28

Olympic medals have been won by US swimmer Michael Phelps including 23 gold – the most of any competitor.

23 years separate Birgit Fischer winning her first Olympic gold medal in canoeing at the age of 18 and her last when she was 42. Fischer won eight Olympic golds in total, and holds the record for both the youngest and oldest canoeing champion.

MEXICO AND CENTRAL AMERICA

Mexico is just north of the seven countries that form the region called Central America. Out in the Caribbean Sea, hundreds of islands make up more than 25 nations or dependencies, from Cuba with a population of 11.25 million to tiny Montserrat, home to just 5,000 people.

4,800 is the number of times per minute a bee hummingbird can beat its wings!

30 tubes of toothpaste are used by Mexican artist Cristiam Ramos to paint a portrait of a celebrity such as Miley Cyrus, Beyonce, or Lady Gaga.

Ramos' portraits can take up to 200 hours to complete.

3.9 inches is the length of the Barbados threadsnake, the world's smallest snake species.

4:34 is the number of minutes and seconds that New Zealander William Trubridge held his breath as he dived down 407 feet at Dean's Blue Hole off the coast of the Bahamas in May 2016.

179.6-196.7 degrees Fahrenheit is the temperature range of the water around the edge of Dominica's Boiling Lake. The lake is in the middle of a rainforest and is heated by hot rocks from a crack in Earth's crust.

198 pounds of sand is produced by a single adult parrotfish in a year. Parrotfish eat seaweed and tiny coral polyps. They poop out the coral as white sand that fringes many islands in the Caribbean.

7.38

feet is the maximum wingspan of Panama's national bird, the harpy eagle. The most powerful bird of prey in the Americas, female harpy eagles can grow up to 20 pounds in weight.

3.8

inches is the height of the smallest adult dog, a chihuahua called Milly. Milly is a particularly pint-size pooch who lives in Puerto Rico and weighs less than 17.6 ounces.

1,728

pounds is the weight of the world's biggest pretzel, baked in El Salvador in 2015. It was 29.3 by 13.3 feet.

2,976,240

tons of pineapples were grown in 2013 in Costa Rica, the world's leading producer.

11,904,960

pounds of silver was mined in Mexico in 2015. Mexico is the world's leading producer, providing nearly 20 percent of all the world's silver.

295

feet was the depth of the sinkhole that suddenly appeared in Guatemala City in 2010. The hole, as deep as some 30-story buildings, swallowed a factory.

Wrecks and Treasure

Journey below the crashing ocean waves to discover mind-boggling numbers from around the world about shipwrecks, rocket engines, underwater villages, gold, gems, and much, much more.

360,000 is the number of bombs that are thought to be on board the *Umbria*, which was used to transport bombs during World War II until it sank in the Red Sea.

5 people lived in an underwater village, Conshelf II, for a month in 1963. Located in the Red Sea, it was designed by the famous underwater explorer Jacques Cousteau. The remains of the village are still on the seabed.

44 years after their 1969 journey into space, the engines used to launch the Apollo 11 mission to the Moon were found in the Atlantic Ocean.

3,000,000 shipwrecks are thought to be spread across the ocean floors.

The Apollo 11 rocket engines were found in pieces on the ocean floor during a 2013 expedition.

22,000,000

160

minutes is the time it took the *Titanic* to sink after hitting an iceberg on her maiden voyage in 1912.

24,640

dives were made between 1979 and 1982 to recover more than 19,000 objects from the sunken Tudor warship, the *Mary Rose*. The ship sank in 1545, near the south coast of England.

18,904

feet below sea level is where the deepest known shipwreck was discovered by an underwater robot in 1996. It is the *SS Rio Grande*, which sank in 1944 in the South Atlantic Ocean.

200

chests of gems are thought to have been on board the *Flor de la Mar* when it sank off the coast of the Indonesian island of Sumatra in 1511, but this ship has never been found!

tons of gold are believed to be in the ocean. Most of the metal is dissolved in the seawater, but some is on the seafloor.

SOUTH AMERICA

South America is a wonderland of fabulous plants and creatures that live in its rugged Andean mountain range or deserts, plains, and lush rainforest. The 12 countries that make up most of its land range from Brazil – the fifth largest country in the world – to Suriname, which is 50 times smaller.

16,000

fireworks exploded in one evening in the Chilean city of Valparaiso in 2007. This giant firework display celebrated the arrival of the New Year and was one of the biggest ever in South America.

7,065

is the approximate age of the oldest Chinchorro mummy found in Chile. The Chinchorro people made mummies more than 2,000 years before the ancient Egyptians.

1

day is how long a prisoner in Arisvaldo

11

billion tons of salt are believed to lie in the biggest salt flats in the world – Salar de Uyuni in Bolivia. With an area of 4,086 square miles, these salt flats are bigger than the island of Cyprus.

69

is the number of days 33 miners (32 from Chile and one from Bolivia) were trapped 2,257 feet underground after the collapse of the San José Mine in Chile in 2010. The miners were all rescued.

121

feet (about the length of three school buses) is the estimated length of the largest dinosaur fossil, found in Argentina in 2014. The dinosaur, named Titanosaurus, was a plant eater that consumed more than a dumpster full of plants each day and weighed around 77 tons.

587 parades took place in Rio de Janeiro during the Rio Carnival in 2015. The carnival is the biggest street party in the world, attended by around 5 million Brazilians and foreign visitors.

25 percent of the world's coffee beans are produced in Brazil.

de Campos Pires jail in Brazil gets taken off their prison sentence for every three days they spend knitting!

11 inches is the leg span of a male goliath bird-eating spider. The spider is as big as a dinner plate.

2,500,000 different insect species can be found in the Amazon rainforest. There are also more than 1,300 different types of bird and over 3,000 species of fish.

Goliath spiders feast on toads, lizards, snakes and small birds.

160 is the number of times that a giant anteater can flick its 23.6-inch tongue in and out of its mouth every minute when eating ants, termites, and other insects.

20 percent of all the fresh water that flows into the world's seas and oceans comes from the Amazon river. The Amazon is more than 3,728 miles long and is fed by waters from more than 1,000 smaller rivers.

AUSTRALASIA

This fascinating region of the world is mostly water (the Pacific Ocean), but it is also dotted with more than 25,000 islands. Most are small, but Australia is BIG. You could fit the United Kingdom into Australia 31 times and still have space left over.

18
hours a day is the amount of time that koalas can sleep.

9,142
square miles is the area of the biggest cattle ranch in Australia. Anna Creek cattle station is bigger than Israel and over half the size of the country of Denmark.

29.5
million sheep live in New Zealand. There are more than six sheep for every person living in the country.

97
pounds is the weight of the homemade suit of armor worn by notorious Australian outlaw Ned Kelly (1854–1880). The armor was made from thick iron plates taken from farm plows.

29.53
feet is the distance a male red kangaroo can leap in a single bound. Growing up to 5.25 feet tall with a tail as long as 3.61 feet, the red kangaroo is the largest marsupial in the world.

102
cane toads from South America were introduced into Australia in 1935 to help control the spread of a beetle that ate sugar cane crops. There are more than 200 million toads today!

211

is the average number of landings the Royal Flying Doctor Service made per day in 2015. They travelled 45,704 miles and treated 800 patients every day.

887

giant stone heads, called moai, were carved by the Rapa Nui people on tiny Easter Island in the Pacific Ocean. The largest completed statue weighs 82 tons and stands 32.15 feet high.

15,500

is the number of light bulbs changed every year at the Sydney Opera House. The giant building's many halls and rooms host around 3,000 arts and music events each year.

10,685

beaches are found around the coast of Australia. If you went to a different beach each day, it would take you 29 years and 3 months to visit them all.

1,625

is the total number of different species of fish found living on the Great Barrier Reef, including the 23-foot-wide manta ray.

The Great Barrier Reef is also home to 6 species of turtles, 14 species of sea snakes, and 100 species of jellyfish.

Amazing Journeys

In 1895, there were just 300 motor cars produced in the whole of the USA. By 2014, that number had risen to 260,350,938 cars, motorbikes, and buses. Today, millions of other vehicles such as planes, boats, ships, and bicycles whisk people off on journeys all over the world.

1 railway station in the African country of Lesotho is the only stop on 0.99 miles of track linking it to South Africa.

23 million passengers are carried every day by trains in India. That's almost equal to the entire population of Australia.

251 men and 11 motorcycles formed the biggest ever motorcycle pyramid. The Indian Army Signals Corp traveled 787 feet in New Delhi in 2008.

120 inches is the height of each of the tires fitted to the Bigfoot 5 monster truck. Each tire weighs over 2,200 pounds, and the entire truck weighs about 14 tons — more than two adult elephants.

8,500

eggs are consumed every day by the 7,000 passengers and crew on board the world's biggest cruise ship, the *Harmony of the Seas*. The 1,188-foot-long ship has a theater, ice rink, and 23 pools.

21

days is the time it takes for the world's longest single railway journey. The train runs between the Chinese city of Yiwu through China, Kazakhstan, Russia, Belarus, Poland, Germany, and France to the Spanish city of Madrid.

2,255

feet is the distance that Sam Tartamella traveled on his skateboard in 1996 . . . while performing a handstand!

124

days was the length of time that it took Pete McDonald to cross the entire USA on stilts. McDonald walked 3,200 miles on his 26-inch stilts.

6,000,000

parts make up a Boeing 747 airliner. That's 200 times the number found in a typical car. These aircraft have flown almost 50 billion miles – equivalent to more than 73,000 trips to the Moon and back!

367

miles per hour is the speed of the world's fastest school bus. The bus is fitted with a jet engine from a Phantom military aircraft and uses 150 gallons of fuel to travel just 1,319 feet.

THE POLES

Around four million people in Canada, Alaska, Greenland, Finland, Norway, Sweden, and Russia live inside the Arctic Circle with its long winters. It's even colder in Antarctica, home of the South Pole. The warmest temperature there is minus 9.86 degrees Fahrenheit . . . brrrr!

21 dogs lead a sled racing team at the start of the Iditarod, a famous dog sled race run over 994 miles of snow and ice in Alaska every year.

The race was won in 2016 by Dallas Seavey in 8 days, 11 hours, and 20 minutes.

89 was the age of the oldest person to reach the North Pole. Dorothy Davenhill Hirsch was 89 years and 109 days old when she reached the North Pole in 2004 on board the Russian icebreaker *Yamal*.

NORTH POLE

4,000 is the number of clams and other shellfish a single walrus can eat in one feeding session. No wonder these large creatures, covered in a 6-inch-thick layer of blubber to insulate them from the Arctic cold, like a long nap after dinner. Walruses have been known to sleep for 19 hours!

1,320 pounds is the typical weight of a polar bear, which lives the Arctic. Polar bears are largest hunters on land.

A polar bear can smell a seal more than 3,280 feet away.

121 feet is the length of the tentacles of the largest jellyfish of all, which is found in the Arctic Ocean. The Lion's Mane Jellyfish uses its tentacles to sting its prey.

62

miles is the length of the longest race run on Antarctica. The Antarctic Ice Marathon is run every year, and runners have to battle minus 13 degrees Fahrenheit temperatures and fierce winds.

This crazy race was won in 2015 by Irishman Keith Whyte in a time of 9 hours, 26 minutes, and 2 seconds.

-128.56

degrees Fahrenheit is the temperature recorded in 1983 at Vostok Station, a Russian scientific base in Antarctica. It is the coldest ever recorded on Earth.

SOUTH POLE

16

is the age of the youngest person to trek to the South Pole without dog sleds or motorized vehicles. Amelia Hempleman-Adams skied and pulled a sled alongside her father, David, during their 97-mile-long journey.

MAIL

MAIL

6.59

feet is the length of the biggest penguin ever found. The 37 million-year-old fossil bones of a colossus penguin were discovered on Seymour Island off the coast of Antarctica. The giant bird would have weighed around 253 lbs.

70,000

letters and postcards are franked each year with a special Antarctica stamp at the world's most southerly post office.

Staff at Port Lockroy's post office have no running water or electricity – instead they have 3,000 gentoo penguins as neighbors.

4,247

is the area in square miles of the largest iceberg ever measured. The 183-mile-long iceberg, named B-15, broke away from the Ross Ice Shelf in Antarctica in 2000.

70

percent of all fresh water on Earth is found in Antarctica, mostly as ice. Despite all that water, Antarctica is Earth's biggest desert, with next-to-no rainfall.